IF FOI

👤 _____

✉ _____

📱 _____

Greater Than a Tourist Book Series
Reviews from Readers

I think the series is wonderful and beneficial for tourists to get information before visiting the city.

-Seckin Zumbul, Izmir Turkey

I am a world traveler who has read many trip guides but this one really made a difference for me. I would call it a heartfelt creation of a local guide expert instead of just a guide.

-Susy, Isla Holbox, Mexico

New to the area like me, this is a must have!

-Joe, Bloomington, USA

This is a good series that gets down to it when looking for things to do at your destination without having to read a novel for just a few ideas.

-Rachel, Monterey, USA

Good information to have to plan my trip to this destination.

-Pennie Farrell, Mexico

Great ideas for a port day.

-Mary Martin USA

Aptly titled, you won't just be a tourist after reading this book. You'll be greater than a tourist!

-Alan Warner, Grand Rapids, USA

Even though I only have three days to spend in San Miguel in an upcoming visit, I will use the author's suggestions to guide some of my time there. An easy read - with chapters named to guide me in directions I want to go.

 -Robert Catapano, USA

Great insights from a local perspective! Useful information and a very good value!

 -Sarah, USA

This series provides an in-depth experience through the eyes of a local. Reading these series will help you to travel the city in with confidence and it'll make your journey a unique one.

-Andrew Teoh, Ipoh, Malaysia

>TOURIST

GREATER THAN A TOURIST – SÃO PAULO BRAZIL

50 Travel Tips from a Local

Léia Guimarães S. Carvalho

Greater Than a Tourist- São Paulo Brazil Copyright © 2018 by CZYK Publishing LLC. All Rights Reserved.

All rights reserved. No part of this book may be reproduced in any form or by any electronic or mechanical means including information storage and retrieval systems, without permission in writing from the author. The only exception is by a reviewer, who may quote short excerpts in a review.

Cover designed by: Ivana Stamenkovic

Cover Image: https://pixabay.com/en/river-pines-pollution-city-sewer-2385238/

Edited by: Linda Fitak

CZYK Publishing Since 2011.

Greater Than a Tourist

Visit our website at www.GreaterThanaTourist.com

Lock Haven, PA

All rights reserved.

ISBN: 9781720194804

>TOURIST

50 TRAVEL TIPS FROM A LOCAL

\>TOURIST

BOOK DESCRIPTION

Are you excited about planning your next trip?

Do you want to try something new?

Would you like some guidance from a local?

If you answered yes to any of these questions, then this Greater Than a Tourist book is for you.

Greater Than a Tourist- São Paulo Brazil by Léia Guimarães S. Carvalho offers the inside scoop on São Paulo . Most travel books tell you how to travel like a tourist. Although there is nothing wrong with that, as part of the Greater Than a Tourist series, this book will give you travel tips from someone who has lived at your next travel destination.

In these pages, you will discover advice that will help you throughout your stay. This book will not tell you exact addresses or store hours but instead will give you excitement and knowledge from a local that you may not find in other smaller print travel books.

Travel like a local. Slow down, stay in one place, and get to know the people and the culture. By the time you finish this book, you will be eager and prepared to travel to your next destination.

TABLE OF CONTENTS

GREATER THAN A TOURIST – SÃO PAULO Brazil

BOOK DESCRIPTION

TABLE OF CONTENTS

DEDICATION

ABOUT THE AUTHOR

HOW TO USE THIS BOOK

FROM THE PUBLISHER

OUR STORY

WELCOME TO

> TOURIST

INTRODUCTION

1. Parque do Ibirapuera

2. Pavilhão das Culturas Brasileiras

3. Museu de Arte Contemporânea da Universidade de São Paulo

4. MASP - Museu de Arte de São Paulo

5. Jardim Botânico de São Paulo

6. Parque Estadual da Cantareira

7. Memorial da América Latina
8. Pinacoteca
9. Theatro Municipal
10. Avenida Paulista
11. Catedral da Sé
12. Igreja Nossa Senhora da Consolação
13. Palácio dos Correios
14. Edifício Martinelli
15. Edifício Alexandre Mackenzie
16. Viaduto do Chá
17. Praça Ramos de Azevedo
18. Monumento a Carlos Gomes
19. Monumento a Zumbi dos Palmares
20. Museu do Ipiranga
21. 25 de Março
22. Brás
23. Pátio do Colégio
24. Basílica José de Anchieta
25. Bar Salve Jorge
26. Centro Cultural Casa das Rosas
27. Bar e Lanches Estadão

>TOURIST

28. Little Coffee Shop

29. KOF – King of the Fork

30. Toca do Pirata Restobar

31. Bar do Mané

32. Hambúrguer do Seu Oswaldo

33. Mercado Municipal

34. Tomates Verdes Fritos Restaurante

35. Black Dog

36. Museu de Arte Sacra de São Paulo

37. Feiras Populares de Rua

38. Memorial da Resistência de São Paulo

39. Memorial de 32 - Centro de Estudos José Celestino Bourroul

40. Museu da Imigração do Estado de São Paulo

41. Museu da Polícia Militar do Estado de São Paulo

42. Parque Tenente Siqueira Campos

43. Monumento a Bartolomeu Bueno da Silva

44. Parque Anhanguera

45. Galeria do Rock

46. Monumento às Bandeiras

47. Borba Gato

48. Farol Santander

49. Japan House São Paulo

50. Centro de Tradições Nordestinas

TOP REASONS TO BOOK THIS TRIP

EXTRA HINTS AND TIPS

Bonus Book

50 THINGS TO KNOW ABOUT PACKING LIGHT FOR TRAVEL

Pack the Right Way Every Time

Author: Manidipa Bhattacharyya

About The Author

Introduction

Dedication

The Right Travel Gear

1. Choose Your Travel Gear Carefully

2. Carry The Minimum Number Of Bags

3. Pack One Extra Bag

Clothes & Accessories

4. Plan Ahead

5. Wear That Jacket

6. Mix and Match

7. Choose Your Fabric Wisely

8. Ditch Clothes Pack Underwear

9. Choose Dark Over Light

10. Wear Your Jeans

11. Carry Smart Accessories

12. Learn To Fold Your Garments

13. Wash Your Dirty Laundry

14. Leave Those Towels Behind

15. Use A Compression Bag

Footwear

16. Put On Your Hiking Boots

17. Picking The Right Shoes

18. Stuff Shoes

Toiletries

19. Stashing Toiletries

20. Take Along Tampons

21. Get Pampered Before You Travel

Electronics

22. Lugging Along Electronics

23. Reduce the Number of Chargers

24. Travel Friendly Apps

Travelling With Kids

25. Bring Along the Stroller

26. Bring Only Enough Diapers for Your Trip

27. Take Only A Couple Of Toys

28. Carry Kid Friendly Snacks

29. Games to Carry

30. Let the Kids Carry Their Load

31. Decide on Location for Children to Sleep

32. Get Baby Products Delivered At Your Destination

33. Feeding Needs Of Your Infants

34. Feeding Needs of Your Toddler

35. Picking Clothes for Your Baby

36. Selecting Shoes for Your Baby

37. Keep One Change of Clothes Handy

38. Leave Behind Baby Accessories

39. Carry a Small Load Of Plastic Bags

Pack with a Purpose

40. Packing for Business Trips

41. Packing for A Cruise

\>TOURIST

42. Packing for A Long Trip Over Different Climates

Reduce Some More Weight

43. Leave Precious Things At Home

44. Send Souvenirs by Mail

45. Avoid Carrying Books

Check, Get, Set, Check Again

46. Strategize Before Packing

47. Test Your Luggage

48. Add a Roll Of Duct Tape

49. List of Essential Items

50. Make the Most of Your Trip

Read other

Greater Than a Tourist

Books

Travel Questions

Travel Bucket List

NOTES

DEDICATION

I dedicate this book to my beloved husband Jean A. G. S. Carvalho, my mother Dorva and all those who contribute to improve the city of São Paulo to a better place - and to all travel enthusiasts who come to visit it.

ABOUT THE AUTHOR

Léia Guimarães S. Carvalho holds a degree in Business Administration and works as a writer, content creator and translator - as well as being part of the Multipolarity Studies Center. She is a Brazilian born in Imperatriz, Maranhão; moved to São Paulo in 2014, where she currently lives. She's passionate about travels, mailing, handicraft and cultural knowledge.

HOW TO USE THIS BOOK

The Greater Than a Tourist book series was written by someone who has lived in an area for over three months. The goal of this book is to help travelers either dream or experience different locations by providing opinions from a local. The author has made suggestions based on their own experiences. Please do your own research before traveling to the area in case the suggested places are unavailable.

FROM THE PUBLISHER

Traveling can be one of the most important parts of a person's life. The anticipation and memories that you have are some of the best. As a publisher of the Greater Than a Tourist book series, as well as the popular 50 Things to Know book series, we strive to help you learn about new places, spark your imagination, and inspire you. Wherever you are and whatever you do I wish you safe, fun, and inspiring travel.

Lisa Rusczyk Ed. D.
CZYK Publishing

OUR STORY

Traveling is a passion of the "Greater than a Tourist" series creator. Lisa studied abroad in college, and for their honeymoon Lisa and her husband toured Europe. During her travels to Malta, an older man tried to give her some advice based on his own experience living on the island since he was a young boy. She was not sure if she should talk to the stranger but was interested in his advice. When traveling to some places she was wary to talk to locals because she was afraid that they weren't being genuine. Through her travels, Lisa learned how much locals had to share with tourists. Lisa created the "Greater Than a Tourist" book series to help connect people with locals. A topic that locals are very passionate about sharing.

>TOURIST

WELCOME TO
> TOURIST

>TOURIST

INTRODUCTION

*"The true art of traveling ...
One should always go out on the street like one running away from home,
As if all the ways of the world were open before us.
It does not matter that the commitments, the obligations, are there...
We came from far away, with an open soul and heart singing!"
(Mario Quintana, poem entitled "A Verdadeira Arte de Viajar ")*

In this small book, you will find part of what is best to know, visit and do in São Paulo, an immense Brazilian megalopolis with countless cultures, languages, religions, ethnicities, nationalities and a formidable and enriching history.

Here you will find everything from restaurants, museums, parks, libraries and religious centers to public places and historical monuments, as well as tips on transport options, lodging and other little things that will help you on your trip. Get ready to fall in love with São Paulo - this is sure to be just your first visit because you will want to come back!

I have selected 50 interesting places to visit in the city. Obviously, they do not reflect the totality of an immense and diverse megalopolis such as São Paulo. Many interesting places may not be included here and definitely the list would have to be bigger. However, my idea was to make a short guide to help tourists who visit the city for the first time, or even tourists who visit Sao Paulo frequently, but who may have unwittingly not noticed some important place.

It's important to note that the all 50 tips are from a personal standpoint. That is because I base them on my own experiences. And, since experiences and emotions are deeply personal things, your experiences while visiting the recommendations on this list may vary.

After all, someone visiting a great restaurant with a renowned chef may have the misfortune to receive a meal with too much or too little seasoning, a meat not cooked to their taste, or a warm drink - they are common human errors, even in places of excellence.

Therefore, I have been very careful to select places and attractions that, on average, are quite positive and admittedly good, so that you, as a tourist, have more opportunities to live pleasant experiences and carry good moments in your memories.

>TOURIST

Enjoy the trip, pack your bags and have a good time! Come visit Brazil, come visit São Paulo!

"The True Art of Traveling", in a free translation. Below, the poem in the original version, in Portuguese:

A gente sempre deve sair à rua como quem foge de casa,
Como se estivessem abertos diante de
nós todos os caminhos do mundo.
Não importa que os compromissos, as obrigações, estejam ali...
Chegamos de muito longe,
de alma aberta e o coração cantando!

>TOURIST

1. PARQUE DO IBIRAPUERA

"One of the best parks on the planet"
The Guardian

You'll probably want some greenery (and fresh air) when visiting a megalopolis like São Paulo. Opened in 1954, the Parque do Ibirapuera (Ibirapuera's Park), located in the city's urban area in the Ibirapuera's neighborhood, is the ideal place to rest, practice outdoor activities and socialize with friends or family on a yummy picnic.

You can also take monitored visits with the park staff. Within the park there are numerous places to visit, such as the Pavilhão Japonês (Japanese Pavilion), the Museu Afro Brasil (Afro Brazil Museum), the Ginásio dos Esportes (Sports Gymnasium) and the Monumento das Bandeiras (Banners Monument), as well as many other attractions.

2. PAVILHÃO DAS CULTURAS BRASILEIRAS

Located inside Ibirapuera Park, the Pavilhão das Culturas Brasileiras (Pavilion of Brazilian Cultures) is a museum with a large collection of diverse cultural and ethnic formations in Brazil. It's important to take a deeper look not only at the history of the city of São Paulo, but of Brazilian history as well.

3. MUSEU DE ARTE CONTEMPORÂNEA DA UNIVERSIDADE DE SÃO PAULO

Designed by the famous Brazilian architect Oscar Niemeyer, it is located at Avenida Pedro Álvares Cabral, nº 1301, in the neighborhood of Ibirapuera. Surely you'll want to know a little about the artistic diversity of São Paulo.

A great hint is the Museu de Arte Contemporânea da Universidade de São Paulo (University of São Paulo's Museum of Contemporary Art), which houses national and international artworks and has the largest collection in Latin America, specializing in Western works of the 20th century - a collection of about 10000 works. The Museum is an immense cultural heritage display within this wonderful city. It is worth checking out!

>TOURIST

4. MASP – MUSEU DE ARTE DE SÃO PAULO

Continuing with the Art vibe, another great recommendation for tourists who wish to know more about the artistic part of the city is the famous Museu de Arte de São Paulo (São Paulo Art Museum), better known as MASP. In the MASP building's lower pass (designed by the engineer José Carlos de Figueiredo Ferraz) there is a market-place with many varieties for sale and that is usually held on weekends.

Designed by the Italian-Brazilian architect Lina Bo Bardi, MASP houses a beautiful art collection, as well as hosting several interesting events. It is worth including the Museum in your travel itinerary.

5. JARDIM BOTÂNICO DE SÃO PAULO

Another great option for those who appreciate nature is the Jardim Botânico de São Paulo (São Paulo's Botanical Garden). Run by the São Paulo State Government, the Botanical Garden was designed by the Brazilian naturalist Frederico Carlos Hoehne and inaugurated in 1938.

With an area of 360000 m², the Garden houses about 380 different species of animals (such as sloths, green-billed toucans and howler monkeys) and plants (like xaxins, ferns, orchids, Brazil-wood and several typical plants of the Atlantic Forest), serving as a true place of environmental conservation.

6. PARQUE ESTADUAL DA CANTAREIRA

Continuing our walk through the green part of São Paulo, another great recommendation is the beautiful Parque Estadual da Cantareira (Cantareira State Park). Founded on August 29, 1962, the Park is a Conservation Unit and was declared by UNESCO as part of the "Green Belt Biosphere Reserve of the City of São Paulo" in 1994.

You can visit the park on Saturdays, Sundays and holidays, from 8am to 5pm. It is a true place for the preservation of the Atlantic Forest biome, where you can follow many guided trails, like the Trilha das Águas Claras (Trail of the Clear Waters), spanning almost 700m.

>TOURIST

7. MEMORIAL DA AMÉRICA LATINA

Visiting São Paulo, you will get a taste of Latin America's history. Designed by architect Oscar Niemeyer and founded in 1989, the Memorial da América Latina (Latin American Memorial) is a cultural and historical center dedicated to the integration of the Latin Continent, with political buildings, a library, cultural spaces and several other areas in which various events are held. Visiting the Memorial is an amazing opportunity to gain historical and cultural knowledge.

8. PINACOTECA

The cultural and historical wealth of São Paulo allows for a really large list, and this list definitely needs to include the Pinacoteca of the State of São Paulo.

Opened on December 25, 1905 and designed by the architects Ramos de Azevedo and the Italian-Brazilian Domiziano Rossi, it houses more than 10000 historical pieces, mainly Brazilian paintings made in the 19th and 20th centuries. Among the works of the collection are several of the landmarks of the Brazilian modernist artistic movement.

9. THEATRO MUNICIPAL

The Theatro Municipal (Municipal Theater of São Paulo) is another excellent option for lovers of art and culture. Located downtown, it offers various cultural performances of classical music (and many other styles), dance (classical ballet, contemporary dance) and performances by various artists. Much of the programming is free - or, when events are paid, they are always accessible.

10. AVENIDA PAULISTA

If there is an avenue that represents well the cosmopolitan spirit of the city of São Paulo, this is Avenida Paulista. With many stores, malls, restaurants, bars and kiosks, as well as cultural centers, this is a great place to visit, especially on weekends - if you visit with your children, you can let them have fun with bikes (which you can bring with you or rent through some companies), since the

Avenue stops traffic every weekend for the leisure of pedestrians.

11. CATEDRAL DA SÉ

The immense and diverse religious identity of São Paulo includes the famous Catedral Metropolitana de São Paulo (Metropolitan Cathedral of São Paulo). Known simply as the Catedral da Sé (Cathedral of the See), it was designed by the German architect Maximilian Emil Hehl, who began the construction in 1913; the Cathedral was inaugurated in 1954 and completed in 1967. It's a true historical patrimony and is already part of the city identity. The so-called Praça da Sé (Cathedral Square), just outside the Cathedral, is another immensely famous tourist spot. It's well worth a visit to take a photo on the steps of the church and get a look inside.

12. IGREJA NOSSA SENHORA DA CONSOLAÇÃO

The Igreja Nossa Senhora da Consolação e São João Batista (Church of Our Madonna of Consolation & Saint John the Baptist) is another example of the city's architectural treasures, and its initial construction dates back to 1799. In it, the Irmandade da Consolaçao (Consolation Brotherhood) has always provided shelter and help to the sick and needy.

The church also served as a place to defend human rights and to protect persecuted people during the period of the military dictatorship in Brazil. The beautiful stained glass windows are an added bonus to the visit.

13. PALÁCIO DOS CORREIOS

When we speak of Brazilian national integration, the institution of the Post Office (here know as "Correios" - Empresa Brasileira de Correios e Telégrafos, "Brazilian Post and Telegraph Company") is a point of interest. It's the only organization present in 100% of the municipalities of the country.

When visiting São Paulo, you can know much about the history of Brazilian Post Office and the city itself when visiting the Palácio dos Correios (Post Office Palace), located in the Vale do Anhangabaú (Anhangabaú Valley). Designed by the architect Ramos de Avezeddo and inaugurated on October 10, 1922, the building houses various postal services, stamp and envelope sales, as well as several free historical, cultural and artistic exhibitions.

14. EDIFÍCIO MARTINELLI

São Paulo is the creation of several nationalities, immigrants and peoples who have gathered here. The immigration of Italians formed a large part of the cidde's identity. Inaugurated in 1929, the Martinelli Building, designed by the great businessman Giuseppe Martinelli and designed by the Hungarian architect Vilmos Fillinger, was the highest settlement in the city in his time. It is a historical and architectural landmark of the city, and it remains active with several shops, attractions and a terrace where it is possible to have a great view of the city.

15. EDIFÍCIO ALEXANDRE MACKENZIE

When walking through downtown, it is worth it to visit the Edifício Alexandre Mackenzie (Alexandre Mackenzie Building), better known as Shopping Light.

This historic building, inaugurated in 1929, was home to the old electric power distribution companies São Paulo Tramway, Light and Power Company and the former state-owned company Eletropaulo. Today, it functions as a mall with great coffee, restaurants and snack bars, as well as other souvenirs and products.

16. VIADUTO DO CHÁ

Outside the Shopping Light and Theatro Municipal, it is possible to visit the Viaduto do Chá (Tea Viaduct), the first viaduct built in the city of São Paulo. Idealized by the French Jules Martins and inaugurated on November 6, 1892, it's 204 meters long and is surrounded by several historic buildings and shops. The venue also serves as the setting for several soap operas and television shows.

17. PRAÇA RAMOS DE AZEVEDO

The Praça Ramos de Azevedo (Ramos de Azevedo's Square) is a pleasant environment dedicated to the memory of the architect Francisco de Paula Ramos de Azevedo; inaugurated in 1928, which merges with Rua Barão de Itapetininga, Rua

Conselheiro Crispiniano, Rua Xavier de Toledo, Viaduto do Chá (Tea Viaduct), Vale do Anhangabaú and the Ladeira Esplanada (Esplanade Acclivity). It is worth visiting at night to see the beautiful Fonte dos Desejos (Desires' Fountain).

18. MONUMENTO A CARLOS GOMES

Just above Praça Ramos de Azevedo (Ramos de Azevedo Square), the Monumento a Carlos Gomes (Monument to Carlos Gomes) stands out as an important artistic landmark of the city. Dedicated to the memory of Antônio Carlos Gomes, the greatest Brazilian opera composer (like "O Guarani") and the first composer of the country to have his works presented at Teatro alla Scala, in Italy, the monument is an excellent place to visit.

Antônio had its name inscribed in the Livro dos Heróis e Heroínas da Pátria (Book of Fatherland's Heroes and Heroines), on December 26, 2017.

19. MONUMENTO A ZUMBI DOS PALMARES

Located in Praça Antônio Prado, in downtown São Paulo, the Monumento a Zumbi dos Palmares (Monument to Zumbi dos Palmares) is a landmark in memory of the great Afro-Brazilian icon who fought against slavery, founding the Quilombo dos Palmares as a refuge for escaped slaves. It is an excellent opportunity for cultural and historical learning.

The monument was promoted by the Secretaria Municipal de Promoção da Igualdade Racial (Municipal Secretariat for the Promotion of Racial Equality) to celebrate Black Rights Day on November 20, 2016. The 2m high monument is a work of the artist José Maria dos Santos, a great Brazilian black rights activist.

20. MUSEU DO IPIRANGA

The Museu Paulista da Universidade de São Paulo (University of São Paulo's Paulista Museum), commonly called as Museu do Ipiranga (Ipiranga's Museum) is another amazing point to acquire more culture and historical knowledge. Inaugurated in

1895, it has an immense collection of works, especially from the Brazilian Independence epoch.

21. 25 DE MARÇO

If you want to shop enjoying every penny, São Paulo has the ideal place: the famous Rua 25 de Março (25th March Street). On this street, you'll find shops with utensils, clothes, souvenirs, decorations and even pieces of art, with quite varied and affordable prices, cheaper than other places. The street began back in 1865 and is a historic part of the city. An important tip: be careful with your personal belongings - the place is quite crowded, so thefts are a risk.

22. BRÁS

Just like Rua 25 de Março (25th March Street), there is another cheaper (and with relative quality) option for your purchases: Brás. It's a place with varied clothes and clothing stores in general. The district is in the eastern part of the São Paulo's historic downtown. You can use the Linha Vermelha 3 (Red Line 3) subway to get there. The name comes from José Brás, former owner of the lands where the commercial district is located today. The hint about thefts given about Rua 25 de Março (25th March Street) also applies here.

23. PÁTIO DO COLÉGIO

One of São Paulo's most important landmarks is the Pátio do Colégio (College's Courtyard), outside the Igreja Beato José de Anchieta (Church of the Pious José de Anchieta). It is the starting point of what would later be the actual megalopolis, the terrain chosen to begin the native's introduction to the catechism, an ancient living archaeological place with immeasurable historical value. To step in the College's Courtyard is to set foot on the first steps of the city of São Paulo. In the Courtyard, you can check out a historical bell used by the monks. It is possible to touch it and take pictures in the vicinity. It is an enriching visit - and free.

24. BASÍLICA JOSÉ DE ANCHIETA

The Igreja Beato José de Anchieta (Church of the Pious José de Anchieta), better known just as Basílica José de Anchieta (José de Anchieta Basilica) is the next place to visit after knowing the Patio do Colégio (College's Courtyard). Completed back in 1556, during the Brazil Colony's period, it was the first building erected in the city, back when São Paulo was still just a small village.

St. José de Anchieta was a great missionary of the indigenous people and a prominent Jesuit. The Order of the Jesuits was responsible not only for converting the natives, but also for protecting them against the attacks and expeditions of the bandeirantes (soldiers, mercenaries and explorers whose objective was to capture and enslave people and fugitive African-slaves).

There were several confrontations between Jesuits and bandeirantes with many missionaries ending up being killed. The Jesuits, among them José de Anchieta, were the first group to stand for natives' basic rights and protection. José de Anchieta, by the way, was the author of the first Grammar of the Tupi, the main language of the Brazilian indigenous. When visiting the Basilica, take time to enjoy a Mass (they take place daily at 12:00).

25. BAR SALVE JORGE

The Salve Jorge Bar is an excellent stop in the itinerary of those who want to enjoy a great mixture of good food, good drink and good ambiance. Located at the Praça Antônio Prado (Antônio Prado Square), downtown, it's the ideal place to satisfy your palate - with good company. Important tip: the bar doesn't open on Thursdays. If you want to visit another location, there's also a Salve Jorge Bar in Vila Madalena.

There, you can find typical images of São Jorge (Saint George), as well as references to other personalities with the name Jorge. It's worth visiting to experience the food and to learn a little about the religious and cultural syncretism that exists in Brazil.

26. CENTRO CULTURAL CASA DAS ROSAS

Amid towering buildings of concrete, steel and glass, there is a small refuge: a mansion in the best classical French style, right on Avenida Paulista, number 37, at Paraiso's neighborhood. The Centro Cultural Casa das Rosas – Espaço Haroldo de Campos de Poesia e Literatura (Roses' House

Cultural Center - Haroldo de Campos Space of Poetry and Literature) - in memory of Haroldo Eurico Browne de Campos, an important Brazilian poet and translator -, better known simply as Casa das Rosas, is a space dedicated to culture, art and thought. In it, you will have access to excellent content, especially on poetry and literature. The house is one of the few remnants from the time of the initial occupation of São Paulo, when the city still had a rural and rural atmosphere.

Built in 1935, it was purchased by the São Paulo State government to preserve the property and transform it into a cultural and historical center. They have several public attractions, musical presentations, art exhibitions, libraries and study groups and literary talk events. It runs from 10am to 10pm from Tuesday to Saturday and 10am to 6pm on Sundays and holidays, closed every Monday. It's worth a visit to know more about Brazilian, Brazilian and world poetry.

27. BAR E LANCHES ESTADÃO

If you wish to know something truly "Brazilian" and take a break from fast food, the Bar e Lanches Estadão (popularly known only as "Estadão") is an excellent option. It operates 24 hours a day 7 days a week (it doesn't matter when your hunger appears, you'll be able to enjoy the food at any time of day or night). They serve good food at great prices. Including the traditional Brazilian rice with beans, there are several options for all tastes, like sandwiches, drinks, steaks and the main attraction, the ham sandwich (hailed as the "best in town"). Various political figures, artists and prominent personalities have frequented the place - a simple environment, far from the "gourmet" aesthetics and philosophy, but with an excellent service that can attract all palates.

Active since 1968, the place is an inseparable part of the city and manages to attract clienteles of the most diverse tastes and social levels, from the trainee to the owner of the company and the executive. The Estadão is located in Viaduto Nove de Julho (9th July Viaduct), number 193, at the São Paulo's Downtown.

28. LITTLE COFFEE SHOP

If you want to enjoy a great coffee for a great price, you already have the right place in São Paulo: the Little Coffee Shop. Located at Rua Lisboa, number 257, in the Pinheiros district, it's considered the world's smallest coffee shop.

You're served outside, on the street, so the place is a good option if you want quick service and you're just passing through (the "coffee to go" style) - but there's always an opportunity for a good conversation, and the service is great. In addition to the coffee options, you can also eat delicious desserts such as brownies.

29. KOF – KING OF THE FORK

Located at Artur de Azevedo Street, number 1317, in the Pinheiros district, the King of the Fork (KOF) is an excellent tip for anyone who is cycling around the city. There are cycle paths in the area and the cafe has space to leave the bicycles. On-site, bicycle accessories and coffee-related things are sold, such as strainers (the coffee, made with strainer, here called "coador", is something quite common in Brazil, part of the identity given to the drink here) and filters.

The space is also ideal for those with pets, as it is pet friendly. In addition to the coffee options, they also serve toast with jelly and peanut paste. The space is quite cozy and pleasant. It's worth visiting.

30. TOCA DO PIRATA RESTOBAR

If you want to try the typical Brazilian pastel (mistakenly called "Chinese pastel"), visit the Restobar Toca do Pirata. Among the various options are the cheese, meat, meat with cheese and Portuguese flavors. The atmosphere is quite nice, the service is great (the waiters wear typical pirate clothing) and fast and there are several choices of dishes too.

Even though it's a newly opened space, it's worth a try. It's located at Avenida São João (São João Avenue), number 320, near the Palácio dos Correios (Post Office Palace). They also have a great cocada (a typically Brazilian candy made with coconut and sugar). I highly recommend it!

31. BAR DO MANÉ

The so-called sanduíche de mortadela (mortadella sandwich) is considered the main point of this bar that is already part of São Paulo's identity. The atmosphere is casual and the service is very good. There are several choices of drinks and other snacks, like bolinho de bacalhau (codfish cake), empada and various types of mortadella sandwiches.

Located at Rua da Cantareira (Cantareira Street), at number 306, at São Paulo's downtown, Bar do Mané is a great place to meet the typical Brazilian style bars, unique throughout the world and with a very special identity. The establishment has been operating since 1933 and has both good food and a good story to tell. One quick tip: go there with a hearty appetite, as the sandwiches are quite generous.

32. HAMBÚRGUER DO SEU OSWALDO

Located at Rua Bom Pastor (Bom Pastor Street), number 1657, at Ipiranga's neighborhood, it's another excellent point to know the culture and people of São Paulo. Founded in 1966 by Oswaldo Paolicchi, it's an indispensable part of the travel script for those who want to know the typical cuisine of São Paulo. Today, the place is run by the founder's daughter and heiress, Marta. The traditional recipes remain the same, making their menu one of the best in the city, also serving as inspiration for other establishments.

There are several options of hamburgers and sandwiches, along with drinks such as soda, juices, chicken fillet and hot cheese. Prices are good - but the place is constantly crowded. But here, a full house is a sign that the food is good!

33. MERCADO MUNICIPAL

The Mercado Municipal de São Paulo (São Paulo's Municipal Market), better known simply as "Mercadão", is one of the most significant tourist attractions in the city. Its construction began in 1928 and was completed in 1933. Originally designed by the engineer Felisberto Ranzini, he hired Francisco de Paula Ramos de Azevedo as the architect.

Originally, the place was used to store gunpowder and ammunition; but today it is a great retail place with several options of fruits, meats, fish, cereals, spices, food in general and, of course, several snack bars. With 12600 m² and more than 1500 employees, the market has a daily flow of more than 350 tons of food, traded in more than 290 sales stalls. Every week, it receives a flow of more than 50 thousand people. É um importantíssimo prédio histórico, comercial e um marco arquitetônico da cidade. In the market, you can access the unimaginable Brazilian Brazilians, in addition to the kindness of the countries of the world.

>TOURIST

The Municipal Market is a symbol of the government effort of the 1920s and 1930s to commercially integrate the entire municipality, serving as a symbol of commercial flow and linkage with other production hubs, both within the state of São Paulo and the rest of Brazil (and with many foreign places). It's one of the examples of the cosmopolitan and mercantile spirit of the city. The place is listed as a historical heritage of the city.

34. TOMATES VERDES FRITOS RESTAURANTE

Located on Rua Barão de Paranapiacaba, number 84, in Sé, the establishment has a self-service, grill and several options on the menu - besides soups at wintertime.

The various options of meats, salads, rice, beans and appetizers make up the identity of the restaurants that charge by the weight of the dish (restaurants per kilo), part of the city's identity and culture during lunch hours and breaks at office hours. With around R$35 it's possible to eat an average meal for two people (a very affordable price when compared to other establishments of this kind).

35. BLACK DOG

If there is a typical paulistana food, it is the hot dog (right, the hot dog was not invented here, but that's another story - it gained a special identity in São Paulo). And if there is a brand that represents well the paulista identity of the hot dog, this mark is the Black Dog. Any tourist who likes to eat well should visit one of the points of this national franchise. There are seven points spread around the city: Paulista, Santana, Tatuapé, Pirituba, Água Branca, Santa Cruz and Mooca.

With 16 hot dog options that go far beyond simple sausage bread, the franchise also offers various sizes, flavors, side dishes and bread options and extra portions. In addition, they also sell drinks such as soda and iced tea. And we cannot forget the options of açaí (a typical fruit of the North region of Brazil, well-loved among the paulistanos). It's worth experiencing these delights.

If you want to make a reservation, you can order online. The franchise also has the delivery service in the city.

>TOURIST

36. MUSEU DE ARTE SACRA DE SÃO PAULO

The Museu de Arte Sacra de São Paulo (São Paulo's Museum of Sacred Art) is a true place of historical, social, cultural and artistic learning. It is essential, for any tourist, to visit the place when passing through the city. The Museum is located on the left side of the Mosteiro da Luz (Light's Monastery), a nunnery that was founded in 1774 by Frei Galvão (his remains are buried there), who was the first Brazilian to be canonized by the Vatican. The monastery's architecture is of a colonial style dating from the eighteenth century, with a considerably well-preserved structure. Listed and protected as a historical patrimonial architectural monument, the place is a true refuge within the metropolis, with a rural, bucolic atmosphere.

The Museum, which functions as an "annex" to the Monastery, is maintained by the government of the State of São Paulo and the Archdiocese of São Paulo, and houses an immense collection of paintings, furniture, sculptures and utensils covering a large part of Brazil's history.

Frei Agostinho da Piedade, Frei Agostinho de Jesus, Master Valentim, Almeida Júnior, Mestre

Ataíde and Benedito Calixto are some of the masters and artists whose works are included in the collection. To visit the Museum is to visit some of the identity and historical formations of Brazil and the city of São Paulo. The Museum is located at Avenida Tiradentes (Tiradentes Avenue), number 676, in the district of Luz.

37. FEIRAS POPULARES DE RUA

Street fairs are part of the Brazilian identity. In São Paulo, you can see several of them - and get to know the communities of the environments. There are dozens of popular fairs with different hours of operation (usually open on weekends) and varied options. The typical street fair offers numerous fruit options (banana, mango, grape, lemon, orange, acerola, guava, etc.), the typical cake (here called "cake of the fair") and other snack options (in some of them, you'll find even the typical acarajé, a Brazilian food from Bahia). Prices are always quite affordable, which means that your trip will be worth every penny.

The Prefeitura Municipal de São Paulo (São Paulo's City Hall) offers an online guide (which can also be requested at the city's headquarters) with a list of all the street fairs held in the city, as well as the address and opening hours of each one. Visit one of these fairs and your trip will be worth it!

Important advice: avoid going by car; during these fairs, traffic is blocked in the vicinity and it's difficult to find places to park.

38. MEMORIAL DA RESISTÊNCIA DE SÃO PAULO

From April 1, 1964 to March 15, 1985, Brazil peppered its history with a dictatorship commanded by the military that came to power through "indirect votes", without popular participation. Repression against opposing parties, dissident politicians, critical journalists, artists, thinkers and any "enemy" group members were considered an integral part of the period.

The Military Regime was a period marked by illegal arrests, executions, torture and physical and psychological terror. One of the main centers of official torture was the Departamento de Ordem Política e Social (Department of Political and Social Order), represented in the acronym DOPS. Established for the purpose of coordinating state police in monitoring, intelligence and repression activities, it was widely used during the dictatorship period.

The main DOPS unit was established in São Paulo, at Largo General Osório, number 66, in the Santa Ifigênia neighborhood, in São Paulo. Today, in this place, there is the Memorial de Resistência de São Paulo (Memorial of the Resistance of São Paulo). The old structure of the DOPS has been maintained and transformed into a true museum that takes us back to the time of repression: the cells are still preserved, the windows and doors are the same and it's even possible to check replicas of the prisoners' files that were kept there. There are also expositions with letters sent by the prisoners' wives, friends and children, as well as messages left by them on the cell walls.

The place offers free entry and exhibits. It's an excellent opportunity to know a remarkable (although sad) period of Brazilian history, as well as to feel and imagine the emotions and feelings of those who were there. Important tip: the Memorial doesn't work on Tuesdays. On other days, it opens from 10:00 AM to 5:30 PM (but it 's possible to stay in the place until 6:00 PM).

>TOURIST

39. MEMORIAL DE 32 – CENTRO DE ESTUDOS JOSÉ CELESTINO BOURROUL

Another important historical point to know more about the history of the city of São Paulo and the State of São Paulo is the Memorial de 32 - Centro de Estudos José Celestino Bourroul (Memorial of 32 - José Celestino Bourroul Study Center). Inaugurated on July 9, 2005, the space is dedicated to the memory of the so-called Constitutionalist Revolution of 1932, when the government of the state of São Paulo rebelled against the federal government led by then-President Getúlio Vargas. The aim of the revolt was to overthrow the interim government and convene a Constituent Assembly.

Open to the public with free visitation, the place preserves a great number of equipment, uniforms, objects, weapons, documents and reports of the Revolution of 1932. It is a great opportunity to know more and a history of São Paulo and Brazil. It's located at Rua Benjamin Constant (Benjamin Constant Street), number 158, 4th floor, in the Sé neighborhood.

40. MUSEU DA IMIGRAÇÃO DO ESTADO DE SÃO PAULO

São Paulo is the result of the mixture and convergence of countless cultures, ethnicities, nationalities, religions and worldviews. People from all over the world migrated (in a flow that keeps going on, since people from around the world continue coming to São Paulo) to the city in search of new and better living conditions and, through their experiences, cultures, work and collaboration, made the city what it is today. To know São Paulo is to know a little about the whole world.

The Museu da Imigração do Estado de São Paulo (State of São Paulo's Museum of Immigration) is a space dedicated to the study, memory and conservation of migratory flows, the immigrants' identities and their participation in the historical construction of the city. Inaugurated in 1993 and operating in the building of the extinct Hospedaria dos Imigrantes, it is located at Rua Visconde de Parnaíba (Visconde de Parnaíba Street), number 1316, in the neighborhood of Mooca. In space, content related to migration processes from other countries and locations is also shown.

>TOURIST

When you visit the Museum, you'll have access to a great amount of information about the Japanese, Italian, Portuguese, Bolivian, Spanish, Angolan, Haitian and Syrian and diverse other communities that are now part of São Paulo and Brazil.

Admission is free on Saturdays and, on other days, it costs R$10 (R$5 for students, public education professionals and other beneficiaries). It's possible to make an "online tour" on the institution's official website, knowing the museum in detail - but the visit is indispensable and totally recommended.

41. MUSEU DA POLÍCIA MILITAR DO ESTADO DE SÃO PAULO

Inaugurated in 1958 by Professor Vinício Stein Campos, the Museu de Polícia Militar do Estado de São Paulo (State of São Paulo's Museum of the Military Police) preserves a great historical collection of the São Paulo police institution.

With a collection of about 10.000 pieces, including uniforms, accessories, weapons, medals, furniture, vehicles (including aircraft), military equipment and various documents and records of the history of the institution and the history of the state of São Paulo itself.

From Tuesdays to Fridays, the Museum operates from 9:00 AM to 5:00 PM; on Saturdays, Sundays and holidays, opens from 09:00 to 16:00. The museum operates in a small building, originally designed by the famous architect Ramos de Azevedo to house, at the time, the former Hospital Militar da Força Pública (Public Force's Military Hospital). The Museum is located in a district of military buildings constructed around the former Quartel dos Permanentes (Barracks of the Permanent), where today operates the 1º Batalhão de Policiamento de Choque (1st Shock Police Battalion), popularly known as Batalhão Tobias de Aguiar ("Tobias de Aguiar Battalion").

The Museum also has a library with about 8000 books, in addition to the Historical Archive of the Military Police Museum, open to the public. It is located in Rua Dr. Jorge Miranda, number 308, in the neighborhood of Luz, with easy access.

>TOURIST

42. PARQUE TENENTE SIQUEIRA CAMPOS

If you are a park enthusiast, this is a recommendation that will make it your travel itinerary. The Parque Tenente Siqueira Campos, better known as simply Trianon Park, was designed by the French landscape architect Paul Villon and inaugurated by the urbanist Barry Parker (at a time when the government of São Paulo wanted to follow the trends of the great European metropolises) on 3 April 1892. The Trianon Park followed the style of "garden cities", where green spaces coexisted with the urban environment of the great centers.

Localizado em frente ao Museu de Arte de São Paulo, o MASP, o parque possui uma área de 48,6 mil m², sendo um grande espaço de descanso em meio ao movimento de uma grande cidade. You can reach the park by Rua Peixoto Gomide (Peixoto Gomide Street), number 949, or Avenida Paulista (Paulista Avenue), number 1700.

The park is open every day from 06:00 to 18:00. Admission is free and the space has several monuments, statues, playgrounds, exercise equipment and other attractions, such as the "Fauno Trail" (named after Fauno sculpture by the artist Victor Brecheret

The park opens 7 days a week, from 6:00 am to 6:00 pm, Also, the park has playgrounds, gym equipment and the "Fauno Trail", named due to the presence of the sculpture "Fauno" by the Italian-Brazilian artist Victor Brecheret and the sculpture "Aretusta", by the Brazilian artist Francisco Leopoldo.

In this large space, it's possible to see the conservation of typical species of the Mata Atlântica (Atlantic Forest) and other biomes such as sapucaia, Chinese palm tree, seafórtia, cinnamon, cedar, jequitibá, ironwood, araribá-rosa and several species, totaling about 135 plant species.

The park also houses a number of animal species, such as tortoises, butterflies, seven species of bats and 28 species of birds (such as tico-tico, sage-piriguari), as well as various types of arachnids. Don't worry, none of them are poisonous or dangerous), serving as a place of preservation and reproduction of the species. Enjoy nature amidst the bustle of São Paulo.

>TOURIST

43. MONUMENTO A BARTOLOMEU BUENO DA SILVA

Outside the Parque Trianon (Trianon Park), it's possible to contemplate the magnificent sculpture made in memory of Bartolomeu Bueno da Silva, one of the São Paulo's (and Brazil) most prominent bandeirantes. The sculpture, made by Luigi Brizzollara, is placed on Avenida Paulista (Paulista Avenue) and is part of the iconic urban identity of the city.

Bartolomeu Bueno da Silva, one of the most prominent bandeirantes of the state of São Paulo and Brazil. A sculpture by Luigi Brizzollara is on Paulista Avenue and is part of the iconic urban identity of the city. Better known by the name Anhanguera, Bartolomeu was one of the nine children of Francisco Bueno, which was killed during a confrontation with Jesuits, and Isabel Cardoso. He began to accompany his father on expeditions when he was still twelve. When his father was called to the region of Goiás, Bartolomeu asked the Portuguese king, D. João V, to allow the exploration of gold found by his father and to charge the passage of goods along the rivers of the region. He left São Paulo in 1722 and made a fortune with the gold he had found, and rewarded by the Portuguese Crown with the title of chief captain.

However, as the influence and wealth of Bartolomeu grew, so did the jealousy and hostility of the Portuguese nobility. He was demoted, lost the rights given by the Portuguese king and became increasingly limited to the authority of king's officials, dying in 1740 without poverty, with only one decorative charge.

The monument erected in his memory is a reminder of the adventurers who expanded the Brazilian territory and helped to found the present city of São Paulo, as well as numerous other cities and towns, building the territorial integration from the period in which Brazil was just a Portuguese colony.

44. PARQUE ANHANGUERA

The Parque Anhanguera (Anhanguera Park) is another excellent point for nature lovers, in the district Perus. With 9.5 million square meters, it's impossible to discover the entire Park with just one visit. The park is at Avenida Fortunata Tadiello Natucci (Fortunata Tadiello Natucci Avenue), number 1000 – with free entrance. However, only a few parts of the park are open to visitors, since much of it is

>TOURIST

closed to the public, mainly for better preservation of the local fauna and flora.

In the areas that are open to visitation, it's possible to enjoy cycle tracks, areas for cooper, sports courts and ample picnic areas, as well as campgrounds, party huts and public grills. There are also guided trail options within the park. The park was the result of the purchase of an old farm (Sítio Santa-Fé) acquired by the city of São Paulo in 1978.

Today, it's one of the most important Brazilian areas of environmental conservation, with great fauna (including catingueiros deer, pacas, capybaras, armadillos, skunks, quatis, wild dogs and various species of insects, fish, reptiles and amphibians) - including the immense flora in the park, such as the forests, several national plants and some foreign (like eucalyptus). Well worth a visit - several times.

45. GALERIA DO ROCK

The Centro Comercial Grandes Galerias (Grand Galleries Shopping Center), better known as the Galeria do Rock (Rock Gallery), is a commercial cluster of shops, mostly geared to various rock styles. Whatever your favorite band, you'll probably find some product related to it in one of the many stores in that gallery. There are several attractions at the commercial center, including tattoo studios, clothing stores, music stores, sports shops, souvenir shops (mostly with nerd, geek, hipster themes), stamping (where you can make your custom shirt) and snack bars.

It is worth visiting the terrace of the shopping center, where there is a vegetable garden and a bee care project. The view is a bonus. Inaugurated in 1963, it's located at Avenida São João (São João Avenue), number 439, in the downtown area, between Rua 24 de Maio (24th May Street) and Largo Paysandu (Paysandu's Square). The place also showcases various alternative music projects, local bands and small projects, as well as rock festivals.

The Galeria do Rock is an inseparable part not only of the musical identity of São Paulo, but of the city's own history, as well as of the various musical movements that have made and continue to be part of it.

>TOURIST

46. MONUMENTO ÀS BANDEIRAS

One of Victor Brecheret's works, the immense Monumento às Bandeiras (Monument to the Flags) is an open-air work of art in memory of the bandeirantes and the military expeditions carried out during the Brazilian colonial period, expeditions that were responsible for our territorial expansion and the consolidation of the Portuguese presence in Brazil.

At 11m high, 8.40m wide and 43.80m long, it has a map of the Brazilian territory idealized by Affonso de E. Taunay, showing the routes covered by the military expeditions of the bandeirantes. It began in 1920 and was only completed more than 30 years later, in 1953 - not because of the artist's laziness, but because of several troubled processes in Brazilian politics.

47. BORBA GATO

You will find a statue in honor of Manuel de Borba Gato (better known only as Borba Gato) in the city of São Paulo. He was an important bandeirante of São Paulo, participating in several expeditions with his father-in-law, Fernão Dias Pais. Borba even acquired the position of judge. He died at almost 70 years in 1718 (an age rarely reached at the time).

Son of Sebastiana Rodrigues and João de Borba Gato, he is one of the main names of São Paulo's formation and the territorial expansion of Brazil, since the colonial period. Borba Gato, as well as the image of the bandeirantes in general, is an icon of the symbolism of the spirit of the city of São Paulo: advance, progress, adventurous spirit and entrepreneur. The monument is located at Avenida Santo Amaro (Santo Amaro Avenue), number 5762, in the neighborhood of Santo Amaro.

>TOURIST

48. FAROL SANTANDER

Every great metropolis deserves a good viewpoint so that visitors (and, of course, local people) can enjoy good times with a good background landscape. And São Paulo has the ideal spot for this: the Farol Santander (Santander Lighthouse), inspired by the Empire State). Managed by Banco Santander, it is one of the tallest buildings in Brazil and has several attractions. On the 2nd, 3rd and 5th floors, there is the Espaço Memória (Memory Space), with historical information on the bank's history and the Brazilian (and global) economy; on the 4th floor there is a 360° panoramic view designed by Vik Muniz; on the 26th floor, there is a Suplicy's café (a coffee shop with special coffees, which also serves meals and snacks), decorated in a deco style, and a gazebo, where you can enjoy a great view with an excellent Brazilian coffee.

The place runs from 9am to 8pm from Tuesday to Saturday and from 9am to 7pm on Sundays. It's located at Rua João Brícola (João Brícola Street), number 24, in the city downtown. The visit is paid and can be scheduled with anticipation. But every penny is worth it.

49. JAPAN HOUSE SÃO PAULO

With more than 1.5 million Japanese immigrants and descendants, Brazil is the country with the largest Japanese community outside Japan. They came to the country mainly in the nineteenth century, guided by migration companies, by the Japanese government itself and by promises of prosperity in Brazil - and they built their lives here with various projects and projects that enriched the country. The Japanese community of São Paulo is part of the identity, history and culture of the megalopolis.

Located on Avenida Paulista (Paulista Avenue), number 52, in the neighborhood of Bela Vista, the Japan House São Paulo is a place that registers, values, preserves and expands the memory of the Japanese culture and presence in São Paulo. There, you can find a lot of information about Japanese migrants, their relationship with Brazil and their history, culture, language, traditions and values.

At the House, there are various events about Japanese history, Japanese personalities, cuisine, art, decoration, philosophy and religiosity of the Land of the Rising Sun. The space has a restaurant, several rooms with many attractions (free and paid) and a large bookstore with great titles for purchase. It's

>TOURIST

worth visiting the place and knowing more about Japan, the immigrants, the Japanese-Brazilians, Brazil and São Paulo.

Japan House operates from 10:00 a.m. to 10:00 p.m. from Tuesday to Saturday, from 10:00 a.m. to 6:00 p.m. on Sundays and holidays, and closes every Monday (including holidays). If you want to go to Japan while you are in São Paulo, you do not have to go to the airport, just visit Japan House. Great walking experience with friends, family or even alone.

50. CENTRO DE TRADIÇÕES NORDESTINAS

São Paulo is the confluence of peoples and immigrants from various parts of the world and, of course, from Brazil itself. Practically each one of the buildings that make up the current landscape of the city of São Paulo were built with the help of Northeastern immigrants (here called "nordestinos"). They are men and women who came from states such as Ceará, Bahia, Sergipe, Alagoas, Maranhão, Paraíba, Pernambuco, Rio Grande do Norte and Piauí, and helped to build (literally) São Paulo's identity and wealth, contributing their work, commitment, creativity and energy. Much of the present-day population of São Paulo city is made up of Northeastern immigrants and their descendants.

The Centro de Tradições Nordestinas (Center of Northeastern Traditions), known by the acronym CTN, is the cultural center that brings together the diverse identities, cultures, customs and visions of the peoples of the Northeast. It's a true place of historical and cultural enrichment, with several attractions of the typical gastronomy of this region of Brazil, various events and folkloric representations (such as capoeira, bumba meu boi, forró dances and juninas parties), clothing and handicrafts typical of the Brazilian Northeast.

The CTN is located at Jacofer Street, number 615, in the neighborhood of Limão, in São Paulo. Visit the place during the month of June, during which typical fetivities occur, called Festas Juninas - the food is great and there's a lot of joy and liveliness. To know the CTN in São Paulo is to discover part of the Brazilian Northeastern culture.

>TOURIST

TOP REASONS TO BOOK THIS TRIP

Diversity: you will have access to a small part of what's best in a cosmopolitan, multi-ethnic city full of different nationalities, cultures and religions.

Gastronomy: here, you will know a little of what is exceptional in the city's cuisine and the various options available to try.

History and Culture: get to know various cultural, historical and artistic options that will give you an incredible and enriching experience in every way possible.

>TOURIST

EXTRA HINTS AND TIPS

After knowing 50 interesting places to visit when traveling through São Paulo, it's worth to receive some important tips when you are here. First of all, keep in mind the fact that you'll be in a deeply cosmopolitan city. This means that you will interact with different types of people, groups, identities and cultures. Even among Brazilians, the differences are real: interacting with a paulistano and interacting with a nordestino (northeaster) are very different experiences. Some groups are more open and receptive (like northeasters), others are more closed and reserved (like paulistanos) - even among Brazilians, where the stereotype of camaraderie and joy is very strong, creating a false idea of homogenization.

It's also important to know that although you are in a cosmopolitan city, you will hardly find someone who speaks English among the common people (yes, a lot of people speak English here, but they are still a minority among millions and millions). In most shops, restaurants, and even government buildings, you will have difficulty to find fluent English speakers. Fortunately, despite this, many manuals, government websites, institutional and informational websites come with information in English as well. So, do not worry: you will not have difficulty scheduling visits, tours, trails, etc. But it's good to learn a few basic words and phrases in Portuguese (yes, our official language is Portuguese, not Spanish, as many people think!).

If you need help, you may want to inform yourself by public officials (such as police). Even though many of them do not speak English, they will be able to guide and provide materials that are appropriate for their needs.

Another important point is your safety. We are not in civil war, we do not have serious racial and ethnic conflicts and we do not have extremism or terrorism of religious fundamentalists. This means that regardless of your origin, your skin color and your religion, you will have no problems here. On the contrary, simply being a visitor will make you welcome.

Even so, and unfortunately, Brazil is a very violent country (not in its entirety, since there are places as safe as Europe - or more). I am mainly talking about urban and criminal violence (assaults, robberies, kidnappings, etc.). That means you should take some precautions when you are here. Some simple tips to avoid dangers: Avoid riding with cash, especially in

>TOURIST

large quantities; avoid using expensive belongings; in places of great agglomeration of people, beware of thefts; Avoid walking in certain places (especially certain downtown and outlying locations) at night or very late, and especially beware of approaches from strangers.

These are simple recommendations. Do not be scared! São Paulo is one of the cities with the lowest levels of violence in the world (even when compared to other metropolises). For example, when compared to Rio de Janeiro, the city of São Paulo offers real security. I live here and I realize that. But the extremes live together here: you will see several homeless and beggars (even children), even outside the peripheries.

If there is any need or emergency, use the phones below:

- 190: emergency telephone number to get in direct contact with the police forces.
- 192: SAMU - Serviço de Atendimento Móvel de Urgência's (Emergency Mobile Care Service) emergency telephone number (use in case of accidents, illnesses and anything related to health)

Use this numbers just in cases of need, because fake calls are criminally punished here in Brazil. In Brazil, health and safety services are free. You do not have to pay anything for that. There are private medical services, but your basic health needs will be served by the Brazilian public system.

You will also have no difficulty getting around the city. There are reliable taxi services and you can also use the Uber application (always for safety reasons, taxis are more reliable, although more expensive in general). In addition, there is a whole public transport structure including bus lines, trains and subway with accessible and reasonable passageways by the size of the city and the extension of the service.

Look for information in advance before visiting the sites. Enjoy your trip, short your stay and come back more often! São Paulo is with open arms to welcome you, your friends and your family! Did you like this book? So come and meet these and other magnificent places and attractions of this extremely rich and diverse city!

\>TOURIST

BONUS BOOK

50 THINGS TO KNOW ABOUT PACKING LIGHT FOR TRAVEL

PACK THE RIGHT WAY EVERY TIME

AUTHOR: MANIDIPA BHATTACHARYYA

First Published in 2015 by Dr. Lisa Rusczyk. Copyright 2015. All Rights Reserved. No part of this publication may be reproduced, including scanning and photocopying, or distributed in any form or by any means, electronic or mechanical, or stored in a database or retrieval system without prior written permission from the publisher.

Disclaimer: The publisher has put forth an effort in preparing and arranging this book. The information provided herein by the author is provided "as is". Use this information at your own risk. The publisher is not a licensed doctor. Consult your doctor before engaging in any medical activities. The publisher and author disclaim any liabilities for any loss of profit or commercial or personal damages resulting from the information contained in this book.

Edited by Melanie Howthorne

ABOUT THE AUTHOR

Manidipa Bhattacharyya is a creative writer and editor, with an education in English literature and Linguistics. After working in the IT industry for seven long years she decided to call it quits and follow her heart instead. Manidipa has been ghost writing, editing, proof reading and doing secondary research services for many story tellers and article writers for about three years. She stays in Kolkata, India with her husband and a busy two year old. In her own time Manidipa enjoys travelling, photography and writing flash fiction.

Manidipa believes in travelling light and never carries anything that she couldn't haul herself on a trip. However, travelling with her child changed the scenario. She seemed to carry the entire world with her for the baby on the first two trips. But good sense prevailed and she is again working her way to becoming a light traveler, this time with a kid.

INTRODUCTION

*He who would travel happily
must travel light.*

-Antoine de Saint-Exupéry

Travel takes you to different places from seas and mountains to deserts and much more. In your travels you get to interact with different people and their cultures. You will, however, enjoy the sights and interact positively with these new people even more, if you are travelling light.

When you travel light your mind can be free from worry about your belongings. You do not have to spend precious vacation time waiting for your luggage to arrive after a long flight. There is be no chance of your bags going missing and the best part is that you need not pay a fee for checked baggage.

People who have mastered this art of packing light will root for you to take only one carry-on, wherever you go. However, many people can find it really hard to pack light. More so if you are travelling with children. Differentiating between "must have" and "just in case" items is the starting point. There will be ample shopping avenues at your destination which are just waiting to be explored.

This book will show you 'packing' in a new 'light' – pun intended – and help you to embrace light packing practices for all of your future travels.

Off to packing!

DEDICATION

I dedicate this book to all the travel buffs that I know, who have given me great insights into the contents of their backpacks.

THE RIGHT TRAVEL GEAR

1. CHOOSE YOUR TRAVEL GEAR CAREFULLY

While selecting your travel gear, pick items that are light weight, durable and most importantly, easy to carry. There are cases with wheels so you can drag them along – these are usually on the heavy side because of the trolley. Alternatively a backpack that you can carry comfortably on your back, or even a duffel bag that you can carry easily by hand or sling across your body are also great options. Whatever you choose, one thing to keep in mind is that the luggage itself should not weigh a ton, this will give you the flexibility to bring along one extra pair of shoes if you so desire.

2. CARRY THE MINIMUM NUMBER OF BAGS

Selecting light weight luggage is not everything. You need to restrict the number of bags you carry as well. One carry-on size bag is ideal for light travel. Most carriers allow one cabin baggage plus one purse, handbag or camera bag as long as it slides under the seat in front. So technically, you can carry two items of luggage without checking them in.

3. PACK ONE EXTRA BAG

Always pack one extra empty bag along with your essential items. This could be a very light weight duffel bag or even a sturdy tote bag which takes up minimal space. In the event that you end up buying a lot of souvenirs, you already have a handy bag to stuff all that into and do not have to spend time hunting for an appropriate bag.

I'm very strict with my packing and have everything in its right place. I never change a rule. I hardly use anything in the hotel room. I wheel my own wardrobe in and that's it.

Charlie Watts

CLOTHES & ACCESSORIES

4. PLAN AHEAD

Figure out in advance what you plan to do on your trip. That will help you to pick that one dress you need for the occasion. If you are going to attend a wedding then you have to carry formal wear. If not, you can ditch the gown for something lighter that will be comfortable during long walks or on the beach.

5. WEAR THAT JACKET

Remember that wearing items will not add extra luggage for your air travel. So wear that bulky jacket that you plan to carry for your trip. This saves space and can also help keep you warm during the chilly flight.

6. MIX AND MATCH

Carry clothes that can be interchangeably used to reinvent your look. Find one top that goes well with a couple of pairs of pants or skirts. Use tops, shirts and jackets wisely along with other accessories like a scarf or a stole to create a new look.

7. CHOOSE YOUR FABRIC WISELY

Stuffing clothes in cramped bags definitely takes its toll which results in wrinkles. It is best to carry wrinkle free, synthetic clothes or merino tops. This will eliminate the need for that small iron you usually bring along.

8. DITCH CLOTHES PACK UNDERWEAR

Pack more underwear and socks. These are the things that will give you a fresh feel even if you do not get a chance to wear fresh clothes. Moreover these are easy to wash and can be dried inside the hotel room itself.

9. CHOOSE DARK OVER LIGHT

While picking your clothes choose dark coloured ones. They are easy to colour coordinate and can last longer before needing a wash. Accidental food spills and dirt from the road are less visible on darker clothes.

10. WEAR YOUR JEANS

Take only one pair of Jeans with you, which you should wear on the flight. Remember to pick a pair that can be worn for sightseeing trips and is equally eloquent for dinner. You can add variety by adding light weight cargoes and chinos.

11. CARRY SMART ACCESSORIES

The right accessory can give you a fresh look even with the same old dress. An intelligent neck-piece, a couple of bright scarves, stoles or a sarong can be used in a number of ways to add variety to your clothing. These light weight beauties can double up as a nursing cover, a light blanket, beach wear, a modesty cover for visiting places of worship, and also makes for an enthralling game of peek-a-boo.

12. LEARN TO FOLD YOUR GARMENTS

Seasoned travellers all swear by rolling their clothes for compact and wrinkle free packing. Bundle packing, where you roll the clothes around a central object as if tying it up, is also a popular method of compact and wrinkle free packing. Stacking folded clothes one on top of another is a big no-no as it makes creases extreme and they are difficult to get rid of without ironing.

13. WASH YOUR DIRTY LAUNDRY

One of the ways to avoid carrying loads of clothes is to wash the clothes you carry. At some places you might get to use the laundry services or a Laundromat but if you are in a pinch, best solution is to wash them yourself. If that is the plan then carrying quick drying

>TOURIST

clothes is highly recommended, which most often also happen to be the wrinkle free variety.

14. LEAVE THOSE TOWELS BEHIND

Regular towels take up a lot of space, are heavy and take ages to dry out. If you are staying at hotels they will provide you with towels anyway. If you are travelling to a remote place, where the availability of towels look doubtful, carry a light weight travel towel of viscose material to do the job.

15. USE A COMPRESSION BAG

Compression bags are getting lots of recommendation now days from regular travellers. These are useful for saving space in your luggage when you have to pack bulky dresses. While packing for the return trip, get help from the hotel staff to arrange a vacuum cleaner.

FOOTWEAR

16. PUT ON YOUR HIKING BOOTS

If you have plans to go hiking or trekking during your trip, you will need those bulky hiking boots. The best way to carry them is to wear them on flight to save space and luggage weight. You can remove the boots once inside and be comfortable in your socks.

17. PICKING THE RIGHT SHOES

Shoes are often the bulkiest items, along with being the dainty if you are a female. They need care and take up a lot of space in your luggage. It is advisable therefore to pick shoes very carefully. If you plan to do a lot of walking and site seeing, then wearing a pair of comfortable walking shoes are a must. For more formal occasions you can carry durable, light weight flats which will not take up much space.

18. STUFF SHOES

If you happen to pack a pair of shoes, ensure you utilize their hollow insides. Tuck small items like rolled up socks or belts to save space. They will also be easy to find.

TOILETRIES

19. STASHING TOILETRIES

Carry only absolute necessities. Airline rules dictate that for one carry-on bag, liquids and gels must be in 3.4 ounce (100ml) bottles or less, and must be packed in a one quart zip-lock bag. If you are planning to stay in a hotel, the basic things will be provided for you. It's best is to buy the rest from the local market at your destination.

20. TAKE ALONG TAMPONS

Tampons are a hard to find item in a lot of countries. Figure out how many you need and pack accordingly. For longer stays you can buy them online and have them delivered to where you are staying.

21. GET PAMPERED BEFORE YOU TRAVEL

Some avid travellers suggest getting a pedicure and manicure just the day before travelling. This not only gives you a well kept look, you also save the trouble of packing nail polish. Remember, every little bit of weight reduced adds up.

ELECTRONICS

22. LUGGING ALONG ELECTRONICS

Electronics have a large role to play in our lives today. Most of us cannot imagine our lives away from our phones, laptops or tablets. However while travelling, one must consider the amount of weight these electronics add to our luggage. Thankfully smart phones come along with all the essentials tools like a camera, email access, picture editing tools and more. They are smart to the point of eliminating the need to carry multiple gadgets. Choose a smart phone that suits all your requirements and travel with the world in your palms or pocket.

23. REDUCE THE NUMBER OF CHARGERS

If you do travel with multiple electronic devices, you will have to bear the additional burden of carrying all their chargers too. Check if a single charger can be used for multiple devices. You might also consider investing in a pocket charger. These small devices support multiple devices while keeping you charged on the go.

24. TRAVEL FRIENDLY APPS

Along with smart phones come numerous apps, which are immensely helpful in our travels. You name it and you have an app for it at hand – take pictures, sharing with friends and family, torch to light dark roads, maps, checking flight/train times, find hotels and many other things. Use these smart alternatives to traditional items like books to eliminate weight and save space.

> *I get ideas about what's essential when packing my suitcase.*

-Diane von Furstenberg

TRAVELLING WITH KIDS

25. BRING ALONG THE STROLLER

Kids might enjoy walking for a while but they soon tire out and a stroller is the just the right thing for them to rest in while you continue your tour. Strollers also double duty as a luggage carrier and shopping bag holder. Remember to pick a light weight, easy to handle brand of stroller. Better yet, find out in advance if you can rent a stroller at your destination.

26. BRING ONLY ENOUGH DIAPERS FOR YOUR TRIP

Diapers take up a lot of space and add to the weight of your luggage. Therefore it is advisable to carry just enough diapers to last through the trip and a few for afterwards, till you buy fresh stock at your destination. Unless of course you are travelling to a really remote area, in which case you have no choice but to carry the load. Otherwise diapers are something you will find pretty easily.

27. TAKE ONLY A COUPLE OF TOYS

Children are easily attracted by new things in their environment. While travelling they will find numerous 'new' objects to scrutinize and play with. Packing just one favorite toy is enough, or if there is no favorite toy leave out all of them in favor of stories or imaginary games.

28. CARRY KID FRIENDLY SNACKS

Create a small snack counter in your bag to store away quick bites for those sudden hunger pangs. Depending on the child's age this could include chocolates, raisins, dry fruits, granola bars or biscuits. Also keep a bottle of water handy for your little one. These things do not add much weight and can be adjusted in a handbag or knapsack.

>TOURIST

29. GAMES TO CARRY

Create some travel specific, imaginary games if you have slightly grown up children, like spot the attractions. Keep a coloring book and colors handy for in-flight or hotel time. Apps on your smart phone can keep the children engaged with cartoons and story books. Older children are often entertained by games available on phones or tablets. This cuts the weight of luggage down while keeping the kids entertained.

30. LET THE KIDS CARRY THEIR LOAD

A good thing is to start early sharing of responsibilities. Let your child pick a bag of his or her choice and pack it themselves. Keep tabs on what they are stuffing in their bags by asking if they will be using that item on the trip. It could start out being just an entertainment bag initially but with growing years they will learn to sort the useful from the superfluous. Children as little as four can maneuver a small trolley suitcase like a pro- their experience in pull along toys credit. If you are worried that you may be pulling it for them, you may want to start with a backpack.

31. DECIDE ON LOCATION FOR CHILDREN TO SLEEP

While on a trip you might not always get a crib at your destination, and carrying one will make life all the more difficult. Instead call ahead to see if there are any cribs or roll out beds for children. You may even put blankets on the floor. Weave them a story about camping and they will gladly sleep without any trouble.

32. GET BABY PRODUCTS DELIVERED AT YOUR DESTINATION

If you are absolutely paranoid about not getting your favourite variety of diaper or brand of baby food, check out online stores like amazon.com for services in your destination city. You can buy things online ahead of your travel and get them delivered to your hotel upon arrival.

33. FEEDING NEEDS OF YOUR INFANTS

If you are travelling with a breastfed infant, you save the trouble of carrying bottles and bottle sanitization kits. For special food, or medications, you may need to call ahead to make sure you have a refrigerator where you are staying.

>TOURIST

34. FEEDING NEEDS OF YOUR TODDLER

With the progression from infancy to toddler, their dietary requirements too evolve. You will have to pack some snacks for travelling time. Fresh fruits and vegetables can be purchased at your destination. Most of the cities you travel to in whichever part of the world, will have baby food products and formulas, available at the local drug-store or the supermarket.

35. PICKING CLOTHES FOR YOUR BABY

Contrary to popular belief, babies can do without many changes of clothes. At the most pack 2 outfits per day. Pack mix and match type clothes for your little one as well. Pick things which are comfortable to wear and quick to dry.

36. SELECTING SHOES FOR YOUR BABY

Like outfits, kids can make do with two pairs of comfortable shoes. If you can get some water resistant shoes it will be best. To expedite drying wet shoes, you can stuff newspaper in them then wrap them with newspaper and leave them to dry overnight.

37. KEEP ONE CHANGE OF CLOTHES HANDY

Travelling with kids can be tricky. Keep a change of clothes for the kids and mum handy in your purse or tote bag. This takes a bit of space in your hand luggage but comes extremely handy in case there are any accidents or spills.

38. LEAVE BEHIND BABY ACCESSORIES

Baby accessories like their bed, bath tub, car seat, crib etc. should be left at home. Many hotels provide a crib on request, while car seats can be borrowed from friends or rented. Babies can be given a bath in the hotel sink or even in the adult bath tub with a little bit of water. If you bring a few bath toys, they can be used in the bath, pool, and out of water. They can also be sanitized easily in the sink.

39. CARRY A SMALL LOAD OF PLASTIC BAGS

With children around there are chances of a number of soiled clothes and diapers. These plastic bags help to sort the dirt from the clean inside your big bag. These are very light weight and come in handy to other carry stuff as well at times.

> TOURIST

PACK WITH A PURPOSE

40. PACKING FOR BUSINESS TRIPS

One neutral-colored suit should suffice. It can be paired with different shirts, ties and accessories for different occasions. One pair of black suit pants could be worn with a matching jacket for the office or with a snazzy top for dinner.

41. PACKING FOR A CRUISE

Most cruises have formal dinners, and that formal dress usually takes up a lot of space. However you might find a tuxedo to rent. For women, a short black dress with multiple accessory options will do the trick.

42. PACKING FOR A LONG TRIP OVER DIFFERENT CLIMATES

The secret packing mantra for travel over multiple climates is layering. Layering traps air around your body creating insulation against the cold. The same light t-shirt that is comfortable in a warmer climate can be the innermost layer in a colder climate.

REDUCE SOME MORE WEIGHT

43. LEAVE PRECIOUS THINGS AT HOME

Things that you would hate to lose or get damaged leave them at home. Precious jewelry, expensive gadgets or dresses, could be anything. You will not require these on your trip. Leave them at home and spare the load on your mind.

44. SEND SOUVENIRS BY MAIL

If you have spent all your money on purchasing souvenirs, carrying them back in the same bag that you brought along would be difficult. Either pack everything in another bag and check it in the airport or get everything shipped to your home. Use an international carrier for a secure transit, but this could be more expensive than the checking fees at the airport.

45. AVOID CARRYING BOOKS

Books equal to weight. There are many reading apps which you can download on your smart phone or tab. Plus there are gadgets like Kindle and Nook that are thinner and lighter alternatives to your regular book.

> TOURIST

CHECK, GET, SET, CHECK AGAIN

46. STRATEGIZE BEFORE PACKING

Create a travel list and prepare all that you think you need to carry along. Keep everything on your bed or floor before packing and then think through once again – do I really need that? Any item that meets this question can be avoided. Remove whatever you don't really need and pack the rest.

47. TEST YOUR LUGGAGE

Once you have fully packed for the trip take a test trip with your luggage. Take your bags and go to town for window shopping for an hour. If you enjoy your hour long trip it is good to go, if not, go home and reduce the load some more. Repeat this test till you hit the right weight.

48. ADD A ROLL OF DUCT TAPE

You might wonder why, when this book has been talking about reducing stuff, we're suddenly asking you to pack something totally unusual. This is because when you have limited supplies, duct tape is immensely helpful for small repairs – a broken bag, leaking zip-lock bag, broken sunglasses, you name it and duct tape can fix it, temporarily.

\>TOURIST

49. LIST OF ESSENTIAL ITEMS

Even though the emphasis is on packing light, there are things which have to be carried for any trip. Here is our list of essentials:

- Passport/Visa or any other ID

- Any other paper work that might be required on a trip like permits, hotel reservation confirmations etc.

- Medicines – all your prescription medicines and emergency kit, especially if you are travelling with children

- Medical or vaccination records

- Money in foreign currency if travelling to a different country

- Tickets- Email or Message them to your phone

50. MAKE THE MOST OF YOUR TRIP

Wherever you are going, whatever you hope to do we encourage you to embrace it whole-heartedly. Take in the scenery, the culture and above all, enjoy your time away from home.

READ OTHER GREATER THAN A TOURIST BOOKS

Greater Than a Tourist San Miguel de Allende Guanajuato Mexico: 50 Travel Tips from a Local by Tom Peterson

Greater Than a Tourist – Lake George Area New York USA: 50 Travel Tips from a Local by Janine Hirschklau

Greater Than a Tourist – Monterey California United States: 50 Travel Tips from a Local by Katie Begley

Greater Than a Tourist – Chanai Crete Greece: 50 Travel Tips from a Local by Dimitra Papagrigoraki

Greater Than a Tourist – The Garden Route Western Cape Province South Africa: 50 Travel Tips from a Local by Li-Anne McGregor van Aardt

Greater Than a Tourist – Sevilla Andalusia Spain: 50 Travel Tips from a Local by Gabi Gazon

Greater Than a Tourist – Kota Bharu Kelantan Malaysia: 50 Travel Tips from a Local by Aditi Shukla

Children's Book: Charlie the Cavalier Travels the World by Lisa Rusczyk

>TOURIST

> TOURIST

Visit Greater Than a Tourist for Free Travel Tips
http://GreaterThanATourist.com

Sign up for the Greater Than a Tourist Newsletter for discount days, new books, and travel information:
http://eepurl.com/cxspyf

Follow us on Facebook for tips, images, and ideas:
https://www.facebook.com/GreaterThanATourist

Follow us on Pinterest for travel tips and ideas:
http://pinterest.com/GreaterThanATourist

Follow us on Instagram for beautiful travel images:
http://Instagram.com/GreaterThanATourist

>TOURIST

> TOURIST

Please leave your honest review of this book on Amazon and Goodreads. Please send your feedback to GreaterThanaTourist@gmail.com as we continue to improve the series. We appreciate your positive and constructive feedback. Thank you.

>TOURIST

METRIC CONVERSIONS

TEMPERATURE

- 110° F — 40° C
- 100° F
- 90° F — 30° C
- 80° F
- 70° F — 20° C
- 60° F
- 50° F — 10° C
- 40° F
- 32° F — 0° C
- 20° F
- 10° F — -10° C
- 0° F — -18° C
- -10° F
- -20° F — -30° C

To convert F to C:
Subtract 32, and then multiply by 5/9 or .5555.

To Convert C to F:
Multiply by 1.8 and then add 32.

32F = 0C

LIQUID VOLUME

To Convert:	Multiply by
U.S. Gallons to Liters	3.8
U.S. Liters to Gallons	26
Imperial Gallons to U.S. Gallons	1.2
Imperial Gallons to Liters	4.55
Liters to Imperial Gallons	22

1 Liter = .26 U.S. Gallon
1 U.S. Gallon = 3.8 Liters

DISTANCE

To convert	Multiply by
Inches to Centimeters	2.54
Centimeters to Inches	39
Feet to Meters	.3
Meters to Feet	3.28
Yards to Meters	91
Meters to Yards	1.09
Miles to Kilometers	1.61
Kilometers to Miles	.62

1 Mile = 1.6 km
1 km = .62 Miles

WEIGHT

1 Ounce = .28 Grams
1 Pound = .4555 Kilograms
1 Gram = .04 Ounce
1 Kilogram = 2.2 Pounds

>TOURIST

TRAVEL QUESTIONS

- Do you bring presents home to family or friends after a vacation?
- Do you get motion sick?
- Do you have a favorite billboard?
- Do you know what to do if there is a flat tire?
- Do you like a sun roof open?
- Do you like to eat in the car?
- Do you like to wear sun glasses in the car?
- Do you like toppings on your ice cream?
- Do you use public bathrooms?
- Did you bring your cell phone and does it have power?
- Do you have a form of identification with you?
- Have you ever been pulled over by a cop?
- Have you ever given money to a stranger on a road trip?
- Have you ever taken a road trip with animals?
- Have you ever went on a vacation alone?
- Have you ever run out of gas?

>TOURIST

- If you could move to any place in the world, where would it be?

- If you could travel anywhere in the world, where would you travel?

- If you could travel in any vehicle, which one would it be?

- If you had three things to wish for from a magic genie, what would they be?

- If you have a driver's license, how many times did it take you to pass the test?

- What are you the most afraid of on vacation?

- What do you want to get away from the most when you are on vacation?

- What foods smells bad to you?

- What item do you bring on ever trip with you away from home?

- What makes you sleepy?

- What song would you love to hear on the radio when you're cruising on the highway?

- What travel job would you want the least?

- What will you miss most while you are away from home?

- What is something you always wanted to try?

- What is the best road side attraction that you ever saw?
- What is the farthest distance you ever biked?
- What is the farthest distance you ever walked?
- What is the weirdest thing you needed to buy while on vacation?
- What is your favorite candy?
- What is your favorite color car?
- What is your favorite family vacation?
- What is your favorite food?
- What is your favorite gas station drink or food?
- What is your favorite license plate design?
- What is your favorite restaurant?
- What is your favorite smell?
- What is your favorite song?
- What is your favorite sound that nature makes?
- What is your favorite thing to bring home from a vacation?
- What is your favorite vacation with friends?
- What is your favorite way to relax?
- What is your favorite weather conditions while driving?

>TOURIST

- Where is the farthest place you ever traveled in a car?
- Where is the farthest place you ever went North, South, East and West?
- Where is your favorite place in the world?
- Who is your favorite singer?
- Who taught you how to drive?
- Who will you miss the most while you are away?
- Who if the first person you will contact when you get to your destination?
- Who brought you on your first vacation?
- Who likes to travel the most in your life?
- Would you rather be hot or cold?
- Would you rather drive above, below, or at the speed limited?
- Would you rather drive on a highway or a back road?
- Would you rather go on a train or a boat?
- Would you rather go to the beach or the woods?

TRAVEL BUCKET LIST

1.

2.

3.

4.

5.

6.

7.

8.

9.

10.

\>TOURIST

NOTES

Made in United States
Orlando, FL
02 February 2023

Made in the USA
San Bernardino, CA
09 August 2017

THE END

If you enjoyed this summary, please leave an honest review on Amazon.com…it'd mean a lot to us.

If you haven't already, we encourage you to purchase a copy of the original book.